*First Person Singular*

# First Person Singular

## Worship Through Alice's Looking Glass

### and other Reflections on Worship, Liturgy, and Children

### Carl Schalk

Library of Congress Cataloging-in-Publication Data

Schalk, Carl, 1929-
    First person singular.

ISBN 0-944529-29-1

Book Design by Ruth Lewis
Illustrations by Deborah Seegers

Published by MorningStar Music Publishers
St. Louis, Missouri
Printed in the United States of America

Copyright © 1998 MorningStar Music Publishers
2117 59th Street, St. Louis MO 63110-2800

All rights reserved. No part of this book may be reproduced, stored in a retrieval system, or transmitted, in any form or by any means, mechanical, electronic, recording, photocopying or otherwise, anywhere in the world, without the prior written permission of MorningStar Music Publishers.

*For Aaron, Brian, Peter, and Samuel,
each learning to sing the Lord's song in his own way.*

## *Table of Contents*

| | |
|---|---|
| A Matter of Taste | 11 |
| Again, and Again, and Again | 13 |
| Ambrose, the Children, and Advent | 17 |
| | |
| Baptism and the Small Potatoes | 21 |
| Buzz Words for Our time | 25 |
| | |
| Candles, Children, and an Old Christian Song | 27 |
| Children's Devotions and the Hymn Sandwich | 29 |
| Committing Musical Acts | 31 |
| Cross My Heart | 33 |
| | |
| Do They Get the Best? | 35 |
| Do They Still Have the Cross at Christmas? | 39 |
| Dressing Down for Church | 43 |
| | |
| Growing Up in Worship | 45 |
| | |
| Let's Pretend to a Pre-Recorded Tape | 47 |
| Liturgy and the Plastic Seat Covers | 51 |
| Lord, Now You Let Your Servant Depart | 53 |
| | |
| My Grandfather's Clock and Learning Hymns | 55 |
| | |
| No Fleecy Clouds and Little Lambs | 59 |
| Now Thank We All Our God . . .With Hands | 61 |
| | |
| Reaching High "C" | 63 |
| Real Men Don't Sing | 65 |
| | |
| Silent Times Ahead? | 67 |
| | |
| Teaching the Songs of Faith | 71 |
| Telling the Story | 73 |
| Those Ubiquitous Children's Sermons | 75 |
| Tradition!  Tradition! | 79 |
| Twinkie Tunes with a Ding-Dong Theology | 81 |
| | |
| Welcoming Those Other Strangers | 85 |
| Whatever Happened to the Numinous? | 87 |
| What's In a Name? | 89 |
| Woodsman, Spare that Tree | 91 |
| Worship Through Alice's Looking Glass | 93 |

# Foreword

This is a collection of personal reflections; in the present climate some might call them politically incorrect discourses. They are the result of an invitation some years ago by the editor of *Lutheran Education* to write on topics of my choice generally related to worship, liturgy, hymns, and parish practice, especially as it relates to the nurture and development of children in the life of the church. These short pieces, slightly revised to accommodate a larger readership, originally appeared in that journal under the title "First Person Singular."

In recent years, it has been all too clear that, concerning the worship of the church, "those who know the least about the faith [seem to want to] determine most about its expression," and that in the topsy-turvy Alice-in-Wonderland world in which the worship of many parishes seems to exist, nothing is really as it seems, and words neither mean what they say nor say what they mean. The church itself, not always convinced of the significance and worth of its own tradition, has sometimes been a willing co-conspirator in allowing the social sciences to almost unilaterally shape the agenda, the questions, and ultimately the solutions to what is perceived as a "problem" with worship in our day. Certainly it has been the voices of statisticians and sociologists which have been among the loudest and most vociferous in attempting to determine the shape, form, and practice of worship in our day.

Against that barrage of voices these observations suggest that it is in the celebration of the historic liturgy and in the treasury of the church's song that the church today can find its true roots and the foundation for its efforts to educate and evangelize. These reflections, then, were written in the hope that those who have been so taken by the experimentation of recent years will come to realize the great treasure it has in its liturgy and hymnody. They were written in the hope that they will come to see that, in the words of Garrison Keillor "Some luck lies in not getting what you thought you wanted but getting what you have, which once you have it you may be smart enough to see is what you would have wanted had you known."

Carl Schalk<br>
September 26, 1997

# "A Matter of Taste"

Every day standards and guidelines shape our lives. Without regulations governing food, drink, health, safety, and even the state of the air we breathe, our lives, health, and general well-being would be seriously at risk. Standards for healthy living are a fact of life and are welcomed everywhere.

Everywhere, it seems, except in discussions about the church's worship and its music. There, some say, everyone is entitled to his or her own opinion, no matter how uninformed or harmful such opinions may be. The self-evident connection between the music of worship and spiritual health—affirmed by the Church in every age—is conveniently overlooked.

"It's all a matter of taste." And with that any attempt to establish even basic liturgical or musical standards in parishes goes out the window. One predictable result is the inane concoction of musical and liturgical trivialities served up to many congregations Sunday after Sunday as "relevant and meaningful."

But after all, isn't "beauty in the eye of the beholder?" Erik Routley once commented that "there is no . . . miserable hymn or demoralizing hymn tune, no mawkish anthem or organ voluntary . . . [and, we might add, no insipid setting of the liturgy] but somebody has thought it beautiful." The usual argument in favor of bad music is that fine tunes are without a doubt "musically correct," but people want something simple. In fact, as Routley suggests, the phrase "musically correct" has little meaning; the only "correct" music is that which is beautiful and noble in character. As for simplicity, what could be simpler than *St. Anne* or *Old Hundredth*?

Seeking musical refuge in "what I like" or "what appeals to me" is to withdraw into an individualism which seeks personal gratification before the building up of the *community* of faith. It avoids the simple fact that, in Ralph Vaughan Williams' words, the issue is, first of all, a theological and moral issue rather than a musical one.

It may be one thing, in Vaughan Williams' words, "to dwell in the miasma of the languishing and sentimental hymn tunes [and church music] which often disfigure our services." It is quite another when such an attitude is encouraged by those charged with leadership in worship.

To say, for example, that the choice of hymns in worship is simply ". . . a matter of taste" is ultimately to avoid taking responsibility for the spiritual, musical, and moral development of ourselves and our children.

In matters medical we reject the advice and counsel of our doctor at our own peril.

Regarding worship and its music—for our children's sake if for no other reason—perhaps we should pay less attention to those advocating faddish whims and passing fashions and more to those who can help young and old alike grow into the church's worship, the church's song, and the church's life.

# Again, and Again, and Again . . .

"Tell me again," children say, as we repeat a familiar story for the hundredth time, "Tell me again!" Some stories they know so well that they can say them right along with us. Changing even a word or two brings the instant response, "That's not how it goes."

How do children learn to throw a ball, to jump rope, to tie a knot? Repetition! Not mindless repetition, to be sure, but repetition which ultimately liberates them from concentration on the mechanics and frees them to focus on the joy of doing whatever it is they are doing.

How do children learn to ride a bicycle? By practicing over and over, again and again. Then suddenly—it all falls into place. They are riding! No longer consciously thinking about pumping their legs, keeping their balance, or watching where they are going, all at once it has come together—and they are riding! Free to enjoy the experience without thinking about the individual actions that make it possible.

This is how all of us—children and adults alike—learn to worship. Worship is best when the actions of worship are second nature, when we don't have to consciously be asking ourselves "What do we do now?" As long as we are thinking "What comes next?" or "Do we stand or sit or kneel?" we are not worshipping. We are still learning to worship.

But what would happen if a child who has learned to move the pedals clockwise, suddenly encounters a bicycle where the pedals work counter-clockwise? Confusion, frustration, and the prospect of having to learn all over again how to ride that bicycle. That is why the Church wisely uses the same basic forms and the same wording in its worship again and again. Once learned, they become the stable framework within which both children and adults are set free to concentrate on what they are doing, saying, and singing.

When children—or adults—have learned that their response to the Kyrie bids is "Lord, have mercy," or that they answer the petitions with "Hear our prayer," they participate with confidence. When children—or adults—are confronted each Sunday with new and different forms, there is bound to be confusion. They don't know what to say or do, or whether they should stand, sit, or kneel. In the attempt to fashion liturgies that seem to adults to be "more interesting" or "meaningful," we often place a significant stumbling block in the way of truly meaningful worship.

Children—and adults as well—need a framework for worship which is stable and unchanging. Many so-called "creative" liturgies only foster confusion by constantly changing what we do and how we do it. What some promote as the way to greater participation in worship usually serves only to diminish or squelch participation altogether.

So three cheers for doing worship in the same way week after week. Rather than a numbing monotony, such repetition actually provides a framework within which both children and adults are set free to give full attention to the content of the liturgy, and to catch its fuller impact, significance, and meaning.

"Tell me a story," children say. In the liturgy of the Church we do—the most important story they will ever hear or learn.

And we tell it in the same way—again, and again, and again.

# Ambrose, the Children, and Advent

"Where were the children?"

This partly whimsical thought crossed my mind as I pondered that serendipitous moment in the 4th century which resulted in the introduction of hymn singing into the Western Church.

As the story goes, Ambrose (340-397), the great Bishop of Milan, was having trouble with the Arians, a heretical sect which denied Christ's divinity. When the Empress Justina, who favored the Arians, tried to get Ambrose to open one of the churches—the Basilica Portina—for her adherents, Ambrose adamantly refused. Fearing reprisal from the Empress, Ambrose gathered the faithful in the basilica, singing psalms and hymns to buoy their spirits in this time of persecution. When the soldiers sent by the Empress arrived at the basilica, so tremendous was the effect of the people's song that the soldiers are said to have joined in the singing. The Empress finally was forced to abandon her plans.

St. Augustine, one of Ambrose's converts—who as a young man was present with his mother at the Basilica Portina—wrote some years later in his Confessions about this moving experience and how the singing had made a profound impression on him.

But where were the children?

There were no day-care or early childhood drop-in centers. Were they back home with their grandparents? Augustine's presence with his mother gives us a clue. The children—young and old—were probably right alongside all the other faithful in the church, singing the hymns of faith as they stood with their parents and Ambrose contending for the faith against the demands of the Empress. What did the children sing? Most likely some hymns of Ambrose, those wonderfully rich and sturdy hymns, a few of which are still found in today's hymnals. The children might have been singing some words they didn't quite understand; the melodies might even have been in those "minor keys." But they sang along with all the faithful, their young faith shaped, molded, and nurtured by their song.

Contrast this with Elsie H. Spriggs' comment concerning children's hymns. "There is a modern tendency," she wrote, "to present God as what may be described as a celestial zoo man or an omnipotent St.

Francis. There is a constant stream of hymns about robins, lambs, rabbits, and God's tiny creatures of all kinds."

One does not have to go far to find children's hymns in the "celestial zoo" or "praising God for the daisies" categories.

Take for example:

> *I know that Jesus loved to see*
> *The big trees straight and tall,*
> *The animals and singing birds,*
> *And wayside flowers small.*
>
> *I think he must have loved to play*
> *With kittens weak and frail,*
> *And laughed to see a puppy dog*
> *Try hard to catch his tail.*

Or try this one on for size.

> *I love God's tiny creatures*
> *That wander wild and free,*
> *The coral-coated lady bird,*
> *The velvet humming bee.*
>
> *Shy little flowers in hedge and dyke*
> *That hide themselves away.*
> *God paints them, though they are so small,*
> *God makes them bright and gay.*

Singing and learning strong, solid hymns is crucial in the developing life of young Christians. Good hymns tell the story of the faith, teach theology, and help to incorporate children into the worshipping community. They are vitally important in the shaping and forming of young Christian lives. Perhaps it is time to think again about our use of all those "celestial zoo" and "praising God for the daisies" songs that some seem to think are best for children.

Martin Luther's two hymns for children give us an idea of what he had in mind for children. The first begins:

> *From heaven above to earth I come*
> *To bear good news to every home*
> *Glad tidings of great joy I bring*
> *Whereof I now will say and sing.*

The second, which he specifically called "A Children's Hymn," begins:

> *Lord, keep us steadfast in your Word.*
> *Curb those who by deceit or sword*
> *Would wrest the kingdom from your Son.*
> *And bring to nought all he has done.*

No wimpy "praising God for the daisies" here. No trip through a celestial zoo for Luther.

In the weeks ahead, why not tell the story of Ambrose and the children to your children's choir. Teach them one of Ambrose's finest hymns, memorize it and sing it with your children. You'll find it in most hymnals. In Latin it begins: *Veni Redemptor gentium.*

You may know it better as

> *Savior of the nations, come,*
> *Show yourself the Virgin's son.*
> *Marvel, heaven, wonder, earth.*
> *That our God chose such a birth.*

You couldn't give them a better Advent or Christmas present!

# Baptism and the Small Potatoes

Paraphrasing Garrison Keillor, that doyen of Mid-West common sense: "Christians, left to their own devices, tend to go straight for the small potatoes."

"Small potatoes" pretty well describes a baptism I attended recently. It was done with as little "fuss" as possible. The rite was truncated, apparently to get it over with as quickly as possible. The baptismal font was off in a corner, its placement hardly reflecting the importance of baptism in the Christian community. Water was minimally dabbed or sprinkled, scarcely signing the "drowned and die" motif of baptism. The people—children or adults—had virtually no active part. Instead, they watched the pastor "do something up there."

The operating principle seemed to be: "How little can we do and still have a baptism?" We went for the "small potatoes."

Baptism, we believe, brings forgiveness of sin, life, and salvation, and is the entrance rite into the kingdom of the promise. Luke reminds us that "there will be more joy in heaven over one sinner that repents than over ninety-nine righteous persons who need no repentance." That repentance was necessarily followed by Christian baptism. Do minimalist celebrations of baptism reflect the greatness of heaven's joy? What do such perfunctory celebrations say to our children about its importance in their lives?

The full baptismal rite as celebrated by most Lutherans (other traditions have a similar, though not identical rite) consists of an entrance hymn and the gathering of the baptismal party at the entrance to the chancel, the invocation in the name of the Trinity, receiving the sign of the cross, the Gospel reading, the address to the sponsors, and prayer. Moving to the font, those to be baptized renounce the devil and—together with the entire congregation—confess their new-found faith. They are then washed in the baptismal water, and receive the Holy Spirit in the laying on of hands. The newly-baptized put on a white garment and are presented with the baptismal candle with the injunction to "Live always by the light of Christ." Returning to the altar, prayers are spoken for the one baptized and for their parents, and for all the baptized. The baptismal rite concludes with the announcement of the newly baptized as a member of the Christian community and the welcome by the congregation led by a representative of the community. It is a full, rich rite involving the entire congregation. No "small potatoes" here.

What can be done to restore a fuller celebration of Holy Baptism? For starters, pastors, worship leaders, and congregations might well begin by studying baptism itself and its importance as the great rite of entrance into the Christian community. Such study would include the role of the catechumenate and proper preparation for baptism, the inner dynamics and movement of the rite itself, and the full involvement of the baptismal party, the various leaders in worship, and the entire congregation in the rite. Last of all, we need to take the necessary time in worship to open up to worshippers the riches of the full baptismal rite.

Let's not reflect heaven's "great joy" with a minimalist congregational rite led by worship leaders determined to "get it over with" as soon as possible. Baptism is, after all, a celebration of the whole Christian community, not something simply "done to those baptized."

Let's baptize with the full rite, with a font located to signify baptism's importance, with plenty of water, with all the prayers, with all the singing, with all the "fuss" that the joy and celebration of baptism deserves.

We've settled for the "small potatoes" in baptism long enough. Our congregations and our children deserve much more!

# Buzz Words for Our Time

It's one of the slippery, new buzz words for our time. It replaces such older—and by now largely devalued-modifiers of "worship" as "relevant" "meaningful," and "contemporary." The phrase is *inter-generational worship*. Watch for it cropping up in articles on how to improve worship in your congregation. Watch for it—but beware!

There is a lot to be said for the term "inter-generational worship"—parents, children, grandparents worshipping together. We know that children learn to worship by worshipping. They learn by imitating others, especially their parents and other family members. Children need the experience of watching good role models and imitating them as they learn the liturgy, come to take their rightful part in worship, and grow to understand it more fully. If that is what inter-generational worship is all about I'm for it.

There is also a danger in allowing "inter-generational worship" to become simply another slogan, yet another gimmick, complete with artificial and contrived "participation" in worship. One is beginning to see patently pretentious and transparently self-conscious attempts to involve different generations in worship ("Now let's have all the grandfathers stand up . . .") most of which are not only awkward and inappropriate, but occasionally offensive, and often downright destructive of what the liturgy is all about.

At their best Christians have always encouraged and fostered inter-generational worship.

*We called it going to church together.* Father and mother, children—and if grandparents lived nearby, they joined the family—sitting together in the pews. Children learned from watching their parents participate in worship, they learned what to do, how to conduct themselves, what worship was about. No dropping the children off before church, reading the Sunday paper until church was over, then picking them up again. We went to church together.

*We called it family devotions.* Before or after the evening meal, each day father and mother—grandfather and grandmother if they were present—led in the singing of a hymn, a reading from scripture and a brief devotion, concluding with a short prayer. Children learned to worship as their parents, grandparents, and older siblings provided examples and models.

Certainly attention to "going to church together" as a family and restoring family devotions to a place of prominence in the home deserve a greater emphasis in parish life, worship, and living. If that is what inter-generational worship is all about I wish it success.

But if inter-generational worship is simply another trendy slogan, another slickly packaged gimmick, another frantic attempt to give the impression that "we are doing something to make worship really relevant"—then hold onto your seat and watch out!

# *Candles, Children, and an Old Christian Song*

Families, so all the books tell us, need to do things together. They need to read together, listen to music together, watch TV together, go on hikes, go to the library, go fishing together, or any of a hundred other activities according to their interests and enthusiasms.

Done with any frequency, these activities can easily become "family rituals," stored in their memory banks and in their experience for later recalling and passing on to their children. All these activities become part of their unique "story" as a family. Such rituals to help bind them together.

Christian families are no exception. We need simple rituals to help bind us together as Christian families, both in the home and in the larger family of the church. And in no area of a family's life are simple rituals needed as much as in its worship life.

Christians in the early centuries had one such family ritual which helped them to understand who and whose they were. It was a simple ritual, but one profoundly moving in its simplicity. Each evening as the sun began to set and the light of day faded from sight, Christians in the early centuries would gather together to light their oil lamps and sing a hymn to Christ the Light of the world. The words of this 3rd-century song, one of the oldest Christian hymns we possess, read as follows:

> Joyous light of glory: of the immortal Father; heavenly, holy, blessed Jesus Christ. We have come to the setting of the sun, and we look to the evening light. We sing to God, the Father, Son, and Holy Spirit: You are worthy of being praised with pure voices forever. O Son of God, O Giver of life: the universe proclaims your glory.

The meaning for those early Christians was simple, yet utterly profound. As the light of day faded from sight and the darkness descended, they lit their lamps to remind themselves in song of Christ, the Light of the world, who comes into the darkness of their night to be their Light and their comfort.

Would it not be possible today, at least once a week, even in the midst of busy schedules, to reserve a few minutes to gather the family—

perhaps at the evening meal or at the time of bedtime prayers—and light a candle and sing this ancient song? It would be a powerful reminder of Christ, the Light of the world, who is with us even through the darkness of the night. If sung at the evening meal, the candle might well be kept lit until bedtime and extinguished after the child's prayers before going to sleep.

Such a simple ritual would be a profound and moving experience for children (and adults as well), binding Christian parents and children together in ways many have not yet experienced—regularly reminding them of Christ who is their Light and the center of their life together. It could also help prepare the entire family for participating in the Evening Prayer of the church where this song is sung by the entire family of believers in the congregation.

This ancient song can be found in a variety of forms and translations in most hymnals today. It is often found in hymn form paraphrased as "O Gladsome Light, O Grace," "O Gladsome Light," or "O Gracious Light, Lord Jesus Christ." It is easily learned and sung by children and adults. We might even discover that it is not just for children! It is for all of us, parents and children alike. Try it!

# Children's Devotions and the "Hymn Sandwich"

Most church schools have some kind of regular devotional life. It may be daily devotions in the classroom. It may be a weekly, twice-weekly, or even daily worship for the entire school. Some larger schools gather by age groups (primary, middle, and upper grades) for regular devotions. Sunday Schools usually begin with some kind of devotional exercise.

They run the gamut from excellent to dismal, many adopting the "hymn sandwich" approach (Hymn—Bible reading followed by a little talk—Prayer—Hymn). Teachers or pastors take turns in leading, leaning heavily on a variety of "Children's Chapel Talks" type of material, many consisting largely of cutesy object lessons and moralistic talk.

Can we do better? I think so.

A recently published hymnal* for young students—the best I have seen in a long time —suggests some "rules" for involving children in worship. They are worthy of some thought. Here, freely paraphrased, are some of them.

*Worship in the school or Sunday School setting is always (or should be) in continuity with the worship of the parish.* The church's primary and normal existence—for children or adults—is the worship of the entire parish. A church school does not (or should not) create a liturgical/devotional life apart from the parish liturgy.

*Repetition is not only OK, it is required.* Does a child want a new story read every night? Or a different place to go to bed every night? The same old words, the same old place are a kind of home territory in which the child is set free by the familiar.

*Liturgy is not about how we feel; it is about who we are and whose we are.* Much is made today about feelings and the individual's role in worship. But when we do the liturgy, all this must be balanced with the fact that children and adults are members of a baptized *community*. Hard as it may be for persons in our culture to accept, the liturgy would have us do things whether we feel like it or not. The liturgy does not exist so that I can get my feelings expressed. Rather it rehearses us in the feeling we ought to have. Children cannot be taught this directly. They can only sense it in their community and grow into it.

*Liturgy is something sung.* Why? Why is "Happy Birthday" sung? There are some jobs that the plain speaking voice alone cannot handle; they have something more to express. We need time to dwell on the words. Singing makes that possible.

*Liturgy is like a dance: it involves the whole body.* Posture is part of it. When do we sit, stand, kneel? These are not meaningless directions to be followed. Part of getting the liturgy into our whole being and making it our own, knowing it "by heart", is letting posture flow from attention to the liturgy—not from some spoken direction ("Please stand.") Children and adults can learn that postures in the liturgy are not simply arbitrary physical positions as they reflect on what it means to sit, to stand, to kneel.

*Liturgy is handling and gesturing.* The "dance" that is liturgy is done by everyone. In the liturgy we move, use gestures, carry things. Practicing and rehearsing is important. This does not make liturgy a performance; it is the only thing that can keep it from being a performance. Such simple gestures as folding the hands, the greeting of peace, making the sign of the cross, all such simple gestures are among the little things without which the liturgy will never become the deed of the assembly. We may at first be somewhat self-conscious; but such simple gestures can free us from an undue self-consciousness when we do them all together.

All this suggests that liturgy with children is hindered when we think that "something new every week" is a desirable goal, or that children cannot do much more than sing a few songs.

Let's say good-bye to the "hymn sandwich" approach. We can do better. And the liturgy—as children (and adults) grow into using and loving it—is the vehicle!

**Hymnal for Catholic Students.* Ed. by Gabe Huck. Liturgy Training Publications. Chicago: GIA Publications. Chicago, 1989.

# Committing Musical Acts

Recently I heard a children's choir commit a musical act. As they participated in Evening Prayer, their tone was clear, the musical line sure, the melody sung in tune, the music well-rehearsed. Their preparation seemed thorough and their presentation impeccable.

Children's choirs frequently are notorious for their poor sound, poorly learned material, and poor musicianship in general—for unmusical acts. In many parishes—where a musical act by children is an oxymoron—musicality is often smothered under a blanket of concern for enthusiasm and "participation."

What made the difference between what I had heard that evening—a truly musical act—and what usually passes for children's participation week after week? Let me mention four components which contributed to making the difference.

*The director was well-trained.* Teaching children to sing requires special skills. Not everyone is equipped to do so. Simply relying on well-meaning volunteers who have neither skill nor particular interest ("Someone has to do it!") is hardly enough. We are often too ready to accept good intentions instead of demanding competence.

*The director had a clear concept of the desired sound for the children to achieve.* A director must have a firm concept of the sound the children are to achieve. There are many fine children's choirs which should be emulated. Good recordings abound. Directors of children's choirs will expose their choir to excellent examples and encourage them to imitate the desired sound.

*The director had command of the techniques to achieve desired goals.* Achieving a good sound with children means knowing specific techniques related to breathing, posture, and nurturing a good sound which will achieve those ends. Such techniques, patiently pursued and consistently and persistently applied will inevitably achieve good results. A few tricks learned at a half-day conference cannot transform a motley group of singers into the Vienna Boys Choir overnight. Teaching and learning takes time. Ten minutes at the beginning of Sunday School will not do.

***The director chose music which called forth the children's very best efforts.*** Music which is worthwhile challenges children to achieve the very best of which they are capable. Directors sometimes choose inferior music because they are unacquainted with appropriate literature. Sometimes they believe that it makes no difference to the children, that they cannot respond to beautiful music anyway. Both are certain roads to mediocrity.

If children are to participate meaningfully in the church's song, they must be fed on material which nourishes and inspires—music which challenges and encourages them to commit musical acts. Undisciplined shouting, enthusiastic though it may be, neither inspires nor nourishes anyone. It is certainly not edifying to congregations. Nor does it help young Christians to understand that their best offering is honed, shaped, and developed by disciplined practice and diligent preparation.

More children need to learn how to commit more musical acts in the liturgy. We can help them if we have the resolve to do so.

# Cross My Heart

We see them as an ornament on suits and dresses, perched on top of tall buildings, hanging around the necks of rock stars. Little children still refer to them in the most solemn, binding oath of childhood: "Cross my heart and hope to die, and hope the cat'll spit in your eye."

And in church, of course, where the pastor traces the sign of the cross upon the congregation several times during the liturgy.

It was the beginning of the Lenten season, and, in the course of the Sunday liturgy, the pastor invited the children to come forward to the baptismal font. A large banner showed a figure walking along a road leading to a city in the distance. The figure was Christ, beginning his journey to Jerusalem on the way to his crucifixion. "He was walking," the pastor said, "the way of the cross."

The pastor asked the children about crosses—the ones they drew in crayon in Sunday School, the ones they wore on their coats and dresses, the large cross hanging in the church, the smaller ones on the wall at home.

He reminded them of the cross that had been traced on their bodies when they were baptized, and then showed them how to make the sign of the cross on themselves, tracing a vertical line from forehead to breast, and a horizontal line from one shoulder to the other. The children practiced making the sign of the cross a few times, and the pastor reminded them that as Christians we make the sign of the cross to help us remember our baptism and the Triune God into whose name all Christians are baptized.

In a culture where crosses are everywhere and where few hesitate to use the cross for ornamental, commercial, or artistic purposes, it seems strange that many Christians are hesitant to mark themselves with the cross that was traced upon them at their baptism.

As more people in Christian congregations come from traditions and parishes where making the sign of the cross is a common practice, this custom is becoming more widespread. Is there something we could learn from all this? About our baptism? About ourselves?

I thought about this after the service when I noticed several of the children rather un-self-consciously "practicing" making the sign of the cross, tracing it upon themselves as the pastor had shown them in the service.

"...and a little child shall lead them."(Isaiah 11:6)

# Do They Get the Best?

"Children," we say, "deserve the very best."

And most parents make every effort to see that they get it! There is almost nothing parents won't do to see that their children are given the best that money can buy—the best home, the best bicycle, the newest fads in clothing, and, of course, the very best education. "They're growing, they need to be challenged. Nothing is too good for my children," say Mom and Dad.

In worship, however, we tend to give them the worst.

We give them the worst place in the church building—preferably in the rear where there is nothing to see except the backs of heads. We give them nothing to do—except color or write, anything to keep them quiet. We give them nothing to look at. Unless they are five feet ten inches tall they couldn't see past the folks in front of them anyway.

But worst of all, we give them nothing significant to sing. And when we do give them something to sing, more often than not it is some cloying, maudlin, song with a "religious flavor" so diluted that the flavor is often difficult to detect. What many churches tend to foist on children under the guise of religious song comes dangerously close to pandering. Instead of giving them something to grow into—which is what we attempt, at least, in reading, science, or any other subject that seems to matter—we give them music one can only hope they will quickly grow out of.

"But," someone says, "children can't learn anything better. Besides, they're so cute up there in front when they sing; fidgeting, poking their neighbor and generally amusing us with the preciousness of it. all." Perhaps it is more a case of "visiting the iniquities (or inadequacies) of the fathers (and mothers) upon the children." A river, someone said, seldom rises above its source. If true, then let's raise the source. What is needed is parents and teachers of children—and especially church musicians—who are increasingly sensitive to the simple fact that much which passes for "religious music for children" is just so much theological and musical pap.

Where are those who help prepare children for participation in the liturgy by teaching the hymns to be used for Sunday? Where are those who help children learn even those shorter parts of the music for worship (the "Lord have mercy" responses, for example) which can easily be learned by children and who readily respond on Sunday with "I know that part!" and enthusiastically sing along? Where are those who teach the Gospel Acclamations? The Amens? And so many of the other parts of the liturgy which even young children can readily learn and join in?

They may be there, somewhere, but they don't seem to be much in evidence.

Children, especially young children we are told, learn chiefly through their senses and by doing. Perhaps it's time to bring children up in front of the church where they can see and be a part of what goes on in worship. Perhaps it's time to give them more than crayons and coloring sheets to keep them quiet. Perhaps it is time to bring them to the font for baptisms and to the altar for blessings. Perhaps it is time we teach them to stand, kneel, and sit with the rest of the congregation, to make the sign of the cross, and—most important of all—to begin to teach them the meaning of it all.

"Children," we say, "deserve the very best." Are we really serious? If so, then as far as music to help children really participate in the liturgy is concerned, perhaps—just perhaps—it's time we give it to them!

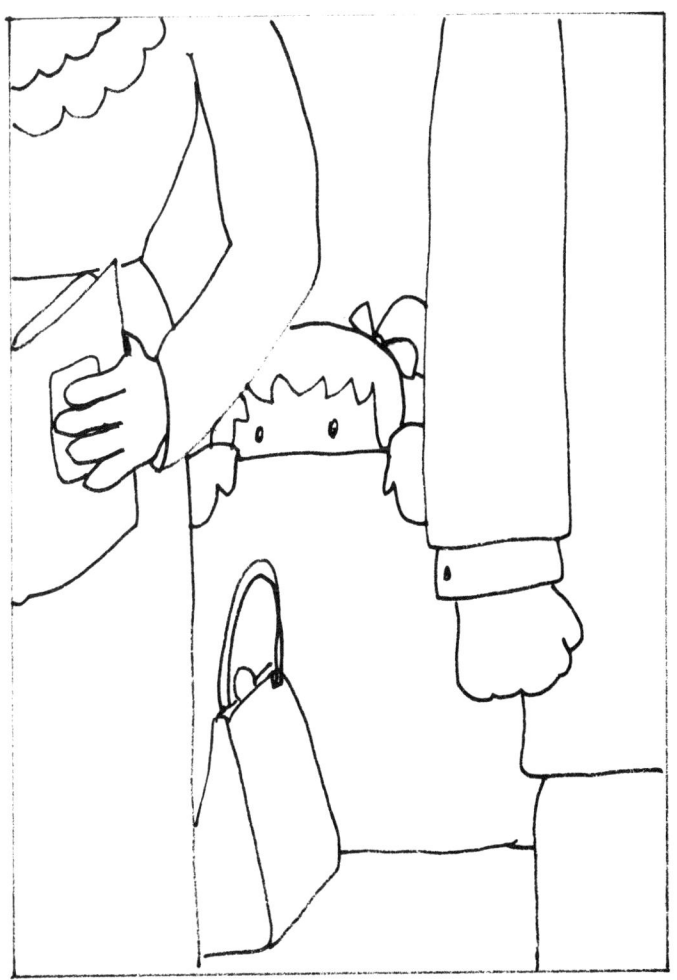

# Do They Still Have the Cross at Christmas?

The choir processes quietly into the dimly lit church, each child holding a lighted candle. Moving slowly and deliberately, their earnest faces reflect the candle light as they sing their familiar carols. Arriving in the chancel, row by row the choir—with candles held high—forms a cross. In the darkened church, glowing in the shape of a cross, the children sing their final song.

> ". . . fall on your knees, O hear the angel voices,
> O night divine, O night when Christ was born . . ."

The children's Christmas Eve service in our parish has begun in just this way for over a quarter of a century. And to be in the choir—to "be in the cross"—is something each child eagerly anticipates as Christmas approaches. Younger children look forward to the time when they too can participate. To be "in the cross" is a solemn moment, one most of them will never forget.

The "tradition" of the lighted cross is one which has been indelibly impressed upon this parish. I would guess it will be going strong long after the 20th century has turned to the 21st. Each of our three children took their place in the cross during their elementary school years. To this day, they and other students returning home for the holidays from other cities, other places, ask, "Do they still have the cross at Christmas?"

But what a strange juxtaposition, the cross and the manger! What is the link that ties together Calvary and Bethlehem? In a beautiful carol written some years ago, Henry L. Letterman made the connection.

> Christmas tree, Calvary,
> Crossing in God's most awesome plan;
> Sin and grace,
> Face to face,
> Bringing together God and man!

He was reminding us that the manger and the cross are both essential parts of God's plan for our redemption. Bethlehem and Calvary can never be separated. Christ was born to die. To separate the manger from the cross is ultimately to sentimentalize the Christmas story leaving us only with "sweet Jesus in the manger with a halo." Our best hymnody has always made the connection, and Letterman's carol does so once again.

This year, by a happy coincidence, engineered by one of our offspring, all our children—now in their thirties—and their families will be home for Christmas. They'll be there on Christmas Eve at the children's service seeing yet another generation of young people "making the cross" and, hopefully, the connection.

Participating this time more vicariously from the pew and not from the chancel, they will be remembering the time when they were "in the cross." And they will be reminding themselves once again—together with the congregation and the choir—of the real meaning of Christmas.

Remembering and reminding themselves—and all of us.

# Dressing Down for Church

There was a time when young and old dressed up for church. Parents, in their "Sunday best," saw to it that pants were pressed, shoes shined, hair combed, dresses starched, and faces freshly scrubbed. Most families had neither fancy or expensive clothes, but the best they had they wore to church.

Today, for many, all that has changed. An aggressive slovenliness seems to have caught the fancy of many young people. Baseball caps, shorts, cut-offs, gym shoes (laces untied, of course), and other modes of dress unthinkable to a former generation are not only common, but tolerated and even encouraged by congregations sponsoring "come as you are" services. Even some adults have adopted a nonchalant attitude, appearing for services in clothes their parents would have been astonished to see accepted as appropriate for worship. Adults—who "dress up" for work—tend to think of church as a time to relax, to be more laid back, to be casual.

About now some pompous pedant is certain to proclaim that God looks only at our heart, not at our clothes, and to denounce the temptations (pride, envy, marking of social position, to name only a few) of church people parading their finery. Let me hasten to agree that God may be worshipped just as readily in a tee shirt as a dress shirt, with scruffy unlaced gym shoes as in polished brogans.

Nevertheless, what we wear for worship undeniable reflects how we understand its importance in our lives. The simple fact is that we all dress up for important occasions. Couples carefully plan what to wear on that special date. They spend time—sometimes an inordinate amount—"getting ready." Those celebrating anniversaries "dress up" to go out. High school proms often demand even more extravagant dress. After all, these are celebrations of important events in life.

In contrast to the laid-back casualness of many suburban churches, there is one place where most people still dress up for church. Visit a typical inner city church on a Sunday. There parents and children alike, many of whom are struggling simply to make ends meet, dress up—often extravagantly—for church. They do so because it is an important event in their lives. And in doing so parents are teaching their children a lesson in what is important for their lives also.

It is certainly true that God looks at the heart. We do not "dress up" for God. But to remind ourselves that what we do in God's house is important, we come in our "Sunday best." We come into the presence of God with reverence and awe to hear his word, celebrate his meal, and to offer our best. That "best" may be the widow's mite, a song of faith, or a simple prayer. It might even include a clean shirt and freshly polished shoes.

# Growing Up in Worship

Young children like to pretend they are adults. When they think no one is watching, girls dress up in their mother's "grown-up" clothes, or try on their mother's makeup. Boys like to hop into the driver's seat of the family car, grab the steering wheel, and pretend to drive. Children are eager to show they are growing up and can do new grown-up things.

And parents are proud to see their children grow and mature. "You'll never guess what little Johnnie can do now," say proud parents to their friends and neighbors. "My, how you've grown," say proud grandparents. Parents are proud of their children and grandchildren as they mature, grow, and learn to do new things. And parents help their children learn what they need to know as they develop and mature, and help them avoid that which stunts or retards their growth.

Everywhere, apparently, but how about in church?

Not that churches are *not* teaching their children. In every parish children are learning about worship. In too many, however, they are learning the wrong things. In some churches they soon discover that real worship is for "adults only" as they are whisked out of the sanctuary to "children's church" elsewhere in the building. In others, they learn by example that, above all else, worship must be fun. They quickly catch on that worship—in many places trivialized beyond belief—is seen essentially as entertainment. And they soon learn that in many churches any serious attempt to teach and nurture children—to help them grow up—in the worship of the Christian community seems to have no place at all.

Many other churches *are* helping young children to grow in worship. More congregation are helping children to participate by teaching them the simple melodies of the liturgy, helping them to learn the songs of God's family in which they, too, can participate. As children from the congregation gather around the font at baptisms, pastors and parishes are helping children learn what baptism means in their lives as well.

As children participate in singing—whether at their parents' side or in parish school choirs—they are beginning to learn the songs of God's people at worship: psalms, hymns, and spiritual songs. In many ways and in many place, parents, teachers, and congregations, by their example and patient teaching, are nurturing children in the worship life of the church.

As parishes begin another year, perhaps it is not too much to ask that the nurture of children in the worship life of the church takes on a new seriousness. For many parishes it is the continuance of a task they have always taken seriously. For others, it will be a seriousness which, in too many places, will be a first.

# "Let's Pretend" To a Pre-Recorded Tape

America's love affair with technology knows no bounds. We are fascinated with gadgets. Slicers, dicers, VCRs, gadgets and gizmos of all kinds find their way into our homes.

Purchased with the best of intentions, they appeal to our highest instincts. They promise to save time, labor, and make work easier. But soon, in many homes, they stand unused, ignored, relegated to the basement, awaiting the next garage sale. They weren't what they seemed to be.

Churches and church music programs, too, are easily seduced by the allure of the latest in technology. ("If God hadn't wanted us to use it, he wouldn't have invented it.") It is attractive because it seems to be the solution to so many of our problems. Of course, technology is not inherently bad. But as its use begins subtly to reshape or misshape our understanding of worship, many of technology's advantages are neither as simple nor as helpful as we may have thought. We easily become captive to its limitations and distortions. Like many remedies, the cure is often worse than the disease.

Enter the pre-recorded music tapes! Containing lush orchestral tracks to be used as background accompaniments to solo or choral renditions sung "live" in the service, they are touted as the latest in "contemporary worship." Born of the "religious-TV" entertainment culture, introduced with little or no thought of the consequences, their unexamined use has had devastating musical results for congregations who have become spectators in an extravaganza of "Let's Pretend."

Congregations can pretend their ten-voice choir is accompanied by something like the Chicago Symphony. Soloists can pretend they are crooning the latest pop Christian hit to the accompaniment of the London Philharmonic.

That most of this music is inappropriate to the liturgy goes unnoticed. That balance and human scale are sacrificed seems to make no difference. That the dynamic aspect of music making—real people making real music—is diminished seems to matter little. (How does one, for example, make the subtle adjustments of mood and tempo, which are part of any dynamic music-making, on a canned pre-recorded tape?)

Effect is everything. And the bigger and splashier the effect the better. Most devastating of all, the congregation's voice is silenced and replaced by pretend music for listening.

Some years ago a popular children's radio program was entitled "Let's Pretend." The word "pretend" means "to affect; feign; to claim or allege insincerely or falsely; make believe." This is exactly what is happening in many churches captivated by the make-believe of pre-recorded tapes.

Let's not teach our children that music for worship is "pretend" music or make believe. Perhaps a first step would be to get back to the human voice, to a human scale, to real people making real music, and music programs that reflect that which can be sustained by the talents and skills of the people of God in a particular place.

That would no longer be "Let's Pretend." That would no longer be pretense striving for effect. That would be teaching children reality.

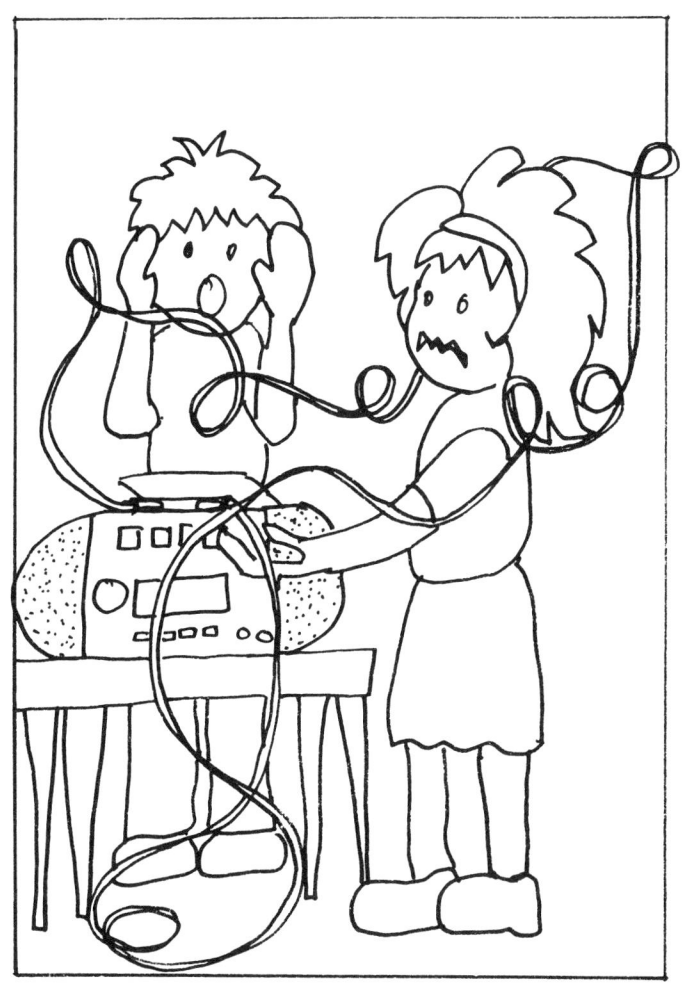

# Liturgy and the Plastic Seat Covers

When I was a young child, I loved to walk the short distance from our house to visit my two favorite aunts. They lived just three blocks away in a small bungalow unpretentiously furnished with plain, modest, practical furniture, yet furniture which struck me—even as a child—as strikingly beautiful in its classic simplicity. One aunt never married; the other had been widowed early in her marriage.

As a ten-year-old I loved to curl up on their marvelous sofa. My favorite among their many pieces of furniture, however, was their wicker table and chairs placed in a little dining area from which we could watch the birds that came to their yard attracted by the small pool, the trees, shrubs, and garden. I spent many hours there as often as possible.

By the 1960s both had died and I was involved in helping break up their home, selling or giving away their treasured possessions, most of which I was convinced was "just a lot of old furniture." We had gotten the idea it was old-fashioned. We didn't need the "old"; what we wanted was something "new," something "modern."

It wasn't so much a conscious decision—rather one in which we unthinkingly moved with the current fashions. So we got rid of their old furniture, including that old wicker table and the chairs in which I had spent many a pleasant hour. Our growing family needed a new kitchen set, and we opted for the stylishly modern: chrome chairs with plastic seats and a table with a formica top.

We soon discovered that our new formica table top and our chairs with the plastic seat covers were neither stylish nor modern. What they were was trendy. And the trouble with trendy, it slowly dawned on us, was that it soon ceased to be trendy, and became something to be discarded and replaced with the next trend.

For some, the liturgy of the church is a lot like that old kitchen set that we so casually discarded. Convinced that it can no longer serve our needs, some are ready to junk our liturgical inheritance like some old furniture which no longer suits the current fashion. It's no longer in vogue. It's not "modern" and so discard it for something that is.

So when I see new approaches to worship touted as "creative," "contemporary," "Spirit-filled," "designed to get your congregation involved," or "to help it grow,"—all euphemisms suggesting that the historic liturgy of the church is old, useless, and ineffective—all I can think of is that plastic-seated kitchen set we bought because we thought it was "modern."

Today our children, now in their 30s and 40s, tease their parents about how they are putting stickers with their names on them on various pieces of our furniture, staking their claim to family "heirlooms" they want to be a part of their family life and "tradition" when we are gone. But its not the "modern" chairs with the plastic seat covers and the table with the formica top they are claiming. It's rather those simple, traditional, unpretentious, practical, yet strikingly beautiful pieces of furniture they grew up with that they want to keep, and have increasingly come to value as part of their heritage, part of our life together as a family.

I think they know something many have forgotten.

# *"Lord, now you let your servant depart..."*

There they were, about a dozen men and women, discussing funerals.

The gathering was a group of senior citizens who met regularly at the church for fellowship, worship, and to hear topics of interest to them. They called themselves the Cornerstone Group, open to all who were living when the church's cornerstone was laid in the 1920s.

The subject was presented by the parish's church musician. The topic was the funeral service, the rite for the Burial of the Dead. But they were not discussing just any funeral service. They were discussing *their* funeral service.

They examined the rite for the Burial of the Dead from the hymnal. They discussed hymns which speak of the resurrection and which have been especially meaningful in their lives. They talked about the particular appropriateness of conducting the burial rite in the parish church rather than in some generic "funeral parlor," the significance and use of the funeral pall which covers the coffin, and the importance of celebrating Holy communion at the funeral.

The organist and choirmaster spoke of the role of music in the service and how the choir might be helpful. Of how the children of the parish school choir were always ready to participate with hymns of comfort and resurrection should families wish it.

They were learning what the church's burial rite had to teach them—and all of us—about life, death, and resurrection. The discussion did not begin and end with "What I want for my funeral service." They spoke freely, openly, and without embarrassment.

In a very real way, they were preparing themselves individually—and as part of the community of the church—for their death and for the final witness they might give to their families, friends, and to the world when the sign of the cross—first made on them at their baptism—would be made on them for the last time as they are laid into the ground.

Here was a group of Christians readying themselves—hearts and minds—for an event for which none of us is ever really prepared. It was a simple, frank, and honest discussion about a subject we will all have to face. And it was welcomed. Not one person present, I am certain, was the same after that conversation.

Such a simple thing to do, yet how often does such a discussion go on in a parish? It is certainly something to think—and talk—about.

# "My Grandfather's Clock" and Learning Hymns

Those who recall the days before television can probably remember when it was not unusual for families to gather around the piano, get out the "Golden Book of Favorite Songs," and spend time just singing together. Many of those songs learned in such homey circumstances have forever embedded themselves in our memories. Songs like "Way Down Upon the Swanee River," "Jeannie with the Light Brown Hair," and my favorite—"My Grandfather's Clock." I can still give it a passable rendition.

That, as they say, was then. This is now. Left to ourselves in this television age, we don't sing much anymore—children or adults—around the piano or anywhere else. Instead, we watch (or listen to) others sing for us. What songs beside "Happy Birthday" can most people really sing at the drop of a hat? And as for hymns?

Not too many decades ago, most children in Lutheran schools learned virtually all the hymns in the hymnal over the eight years of elementary school. Children learned the melodies in music class and learned the words "by heart" as "memory work" in their religious instruction.

Over the course of the elementary school years, learning a new hymn each week, singing it in their daily devotions, and then on Sunday with the whole congregation, many children learned a solid core of hymns which they kept with them throughout their life.

Those days, we say, are gone forever. Today we complain that children can't or won't memorize any more, and if they do, hymns are hardly at the top of their list.

But what are we doing to help them? What standard religious repertoire is being taught in the church's schools, Sunday Schools, or in other parish educational enterprises? Is the hymnal at the center of what we teach? Are we teaching too much trendy material to the neglect of a core of basic hymns?

It is clear that what would be helpful is a comprehensive, systematic, and thorough plan for teaching hymns. Some parishes are working at it with various approaches and varying degrees of success.

One congregation presents to the family of each child baptized a recording of basic hymns to be played, sung, learned, and used at home in the family. Perhaps they are on to something.

Can children really learn a significant body of hymns and religious songs and keep them in their memory for their entire life? The experience of many says "Yes!" But perhaps the best testimony that they can is an old song that keeps running through my mind. I just can't seem to forget it.

"My grandfather's clock was too large for the shelf . . ."

# No Fleecy Clouds and Little Lambs

What makes a hymn good for children?

Answers may vary, but much religious song foisted upon children today suggests that the silly, the puerile, and the childish have taken over. Examples are legion. Generally sensible suggestions which have long served to shape texts and melodies for children have been twisted by current politically correct thought to serve their own ends. The results have generally been disastrous.

Where the simple and childlike is desired, we are given the simplistic and the childish. Writing texts "at a child's level of understanding" seems to result in a general aversion to significant subjects (when have you last sung a children's hymn about death or dying?). Use of repeated melodic and rhythmic figures to aid learning devolves into trite and boring melodies. And where children's voices should soar, we are given low-pitched tunes that encourage the worst kind of sound.

Children are capable of more than this. Our adult cock-sureness of what children like, want, or are capable of, however, has resulted in a patronizing diet of religious junk food being fed to our children in too many churches.

It was not always so. Go back, for example, to Reformation times. The political situation was desperate. The Turks were at the gates of Europe. King Ferdinand had suffered a great defeat at the hands of the Mohammedan Turks at Budapest in 1541. The king of France had made a pact with Suleiman against the empire. Things could hardly have been worse.

In these threatening circumstances there appeared in print a song entitled simply "A Children's Hymn." It was most likely to be sung by the boys choir in a special prayer service. It read as follows:

> Lord, keep us steadfast in your Word;
> Curb those who by deceit or sword
> Would wrest the kingdom from your Son
> And set at naught all he has done.

Lord Jesus Christ, your pow'r make known,
For you are Lord of Lords alone;
Defend your holy Church that we
May sing your praise triumphantly.

O Comforter of priceless worth,
Send peace and unity on earth;
Support us in our final strife
And lead us out of death to life.

Would such a hymn pass the politically correct test for a children's hymn today? No dallying with diminutives ("little Jesus," "little lambs"); no keeping children stuck in a land of "fleecy clouds and little lambs"; no hesitation to address situations of life and death. Besides, what author sensitive to a child's world would attempt to introduce Trinitarian language, or would speak of life, death, and "our final strife" with children? Definitely not for children. Such a hymn would hardly pass muster today.

The author of "A Children's Hymn" was Martin Luther.

In 1542, one year after this hymn was probably written, in a letter to the headmaster of the Torgau Latin School, Luther indicated that he was sending his son John Luther to be drilled in—among other things—music. It is not unlikely that while there Luther's son sang "A Children's Hymn."

Perhaps we might make a start at improving today's situation by teaching it to our children.

# Now Thank We All Our God... with Hands

Like awkward adolescents, most of us just don't know what to do with our hands. Hands often get in the way, which is why we depict someone who is clumsy as unhandy. Hands easily get us into trouble, which is why some parents tell their children to "fold your hands" when praying. We all learn early on that "Idle hands are the devil's workshop."

Martin Rinkart, for one, knew what to do with his hands. Use them, he suggests in his 17th-century hymn text, to thank God for the wondrous things he has done.

> Now thank we all our God,
> With hearts and *hands* and voices.

But how does one thank God with one's hands? At certain times and places we thank and praise God with hands raised in prayer, with hands folded in supplication, or with hands tracing the baptismal sign of the cross. But we also thank and praise God by using hands to do our daily work to the best of our ability.

Today's world often denigrates those who earn their daily bread through "manual labor," at the same time lamenting the fact that competent craftsmen who build and shape are increasingly difficult to find. But even if the modern world deprecates working with one's hands, we cannot escape its vocabulary. The very words we use to describe our lives and activities remind us of the importance of the work of our hands. Parents and teachers "mold" young lives; heredity and environment, we say, "shape" our attitudes; artists "create and form"; we "build" a family; we "carve out" our careers. The vocabulary of laboring with our hands is always with us.

The creation account reminds us that we are God's handiwork—the result of God working with his hands. God "formed" man of dust, "shaping" and "molding" the raw material of earth, breathing into its nostrils, and man being a living being. In our daily work we, in turn, shape, mold, and form the raw materials of this world into works in which God is praised and glorified. Our privilege and responsibility as Christian teachers and parents, as faithful stewards and custodians of the gifts and talents God has placed into our hands, is to be the best teacher, the best parent of which we are capable. And in so doing we are making a profound witness to the world, pointing to the creator of all things who first made us, who first formed us out of the earth.

Into such a world of thought Martin Rinkhart's hymn bursts in to remind us that the wondrous things we do with our hands—our "handiwork"—is a way of thanking and praising God who has first done wondrous things. This is our vocation as Christians: to use our talents, great or small—wherever God places us, to the best of our ability, that the work of our hands may be a labor of thanks and praise to God for all the wondrous things he has done for us.

When we do that we are surely thanking God with our hands. When we do that we are joining the song of the psalmist:

>    . . . establish thou the work of our hands upon
> us, yea the work of our hands establish thou it.

# Reaching High "C"

What teacher hasn't had one of those days when she wonders if it is worth all the time, effort, and hassle? Are the problems of rambunctious students, contentious parents, and uncooperative co-workers ever resolved? Couldn't time be better spent elsewhere?

Then one day—out of the blue—will come a smile, an unexpected hug, perhaps a note from a former student we had almost forgotten—to say "Hello" and expressing thanks for being their teacher. Something we had said or done in a class we had long forgotten struck a spark which started them on the road to the wonders of mathematics or the exhilaration of music. For most of us, it only takes a moment like that to recharge our batteries and renew our strength and dedication.

Those who direct children's choirs know exactly what I'm talking about. A friend of mine—who directs the children's choir of some twenty 10 to 14-year-olds at her church in Northbrook, Illinois, for an hour each Saturday afternoon—is no stranger to the frustrations of leading children into the world of music, worship, and liturgy. As a children's choir director she has, I am sure, put up with her share of unannounced absences, parents who sometimes just don't seem to care, missed entrances, flat notes, uncooperative singers, and the whole range of challenges that are the normal routine of children's choir directors.

In the midst of a catalog of frustrations, she decided one day to count her—and the congregation's—blessings. She decided to simply list some of the *good* things that happened at her weekly Saturday afternoon choir rehearsal last March and share it with her congregation in its monthly newsletter.

Here is her list exactly as she wrote it:

> —a young chorister learned to his amazement that he could reach high C while vocalizing;
>
> —two choir members were given a new descant to read and were able to sing it almost immediately;
>
> —two rather quiet young choristers opened their mouths and made beautiful sounds they hadn't heard before;

—one older chorister whose voice is changing was able to make beautiful, "on pitch" singing while thinking and controlling his voice;

—one chorister who is reluctant to sing solo, sang most of a stanza alone and sang beautifully and strongly;

—the choir learned that on Palm Sunday if the people hadn't sung their alleluias and praise to Jesus the stones would have cried out;

—we sang the words of Isaac Watts: "were the whole realm of nature mine, that were a tribute far too small. Love so amazing, so divine, demands my life, my soul, my all!"

Her comment: "I don't think an hour could have been better spent anywhere."

I couldn't agree more.

# Real Men Don't Sing

What has happened to the singing classroom teacher? Where are the teachers who sing to and with their classes?

One of my abiding memories of elementary school years at Immanuel Lutheran School was the singing. The classrooms were not much different than others of their time. We had no departmentalized instruction, no "music specialists," just one teacher per room who taught everything and a classroom overcrowded (by today's standards) with children.

Every once in a while the teacher would stop whatever we were doing and have us sing—folk songs, fun songs, whatever songs we might know or were learning—for the sheer enjoyment of singing. The last minutes of many days were spent singing hymns, the teacher accompanying us on a well-worn piano. Some of my teachers—not every one, to be sure—could even be heard singing to their classes from time to time. As I recall they were not particularly good singers, but sing they did, to us, for us, and with us—and we with them. We sang with a child's joyful exuberance, without embarrassment. And we loved every minute.

All my elementary teachers were men. The common stereotype has the female teacher singing to and with her children, but surely not the male teacher. Singing isn't something men do. It just isn't macho. Not only don't real men eat quiche, they surely don't sing in the classroom. Well, they did at Immanuel Lutheran School.

But whatever the gender of today's teacher, singing in the classroom is often nonexistent. Wherever those teachers have gone and whatever has happened, it seems that singing in the elementary classroom has suffered a precipitous decline. In schools large enough for a "music specialist" music often becomes just another subject to be learned, and regular classroom teachers can infer that "it is no longer my responsibility." But children learn best by example. And the example of teachers (women *and men*) and parents (mothers *and fathers*) singing to, with, and for their children is a powerful one.

Whatever else we learned in those years, we learned to love to sing. That was a precious gift from teachers almost fifty years ago. It is an equally precious gift that teachers (and parents) can give their children today.

## Silent Times Ahead

When I was a child, it was not uncommon for families—parents, grandparents, and children alike—to gather around the piano and sing. The *Golden Book of Favorite Songs*, the collection of choice, helped establish a repertoire of songs most Americans knew and could sing from memory. Singing was an everyday activity, something families did together, and singing a common repertoire of songs—like "America the Beautiful," "Home on the Range," and "Down by the Riverside"—brought us together.

Today children rarely sing, either at home or school. At home the piano is gone. At school, public or private, singing has been largely abandoned as a normal part of the curriculum, treated at best as an "extra," ready for the chopping block when budgets are tight. Even the national anthem is a song that others sing to us. One can no longer assume that children grow up with a common repertoire of songs—or that they sing at all.

As part of their "Get America Singing Again" campaign, the Music Educators National Conference recently published the following list of 42 songs they feel Americans must continue to learn and sing to preserve an important part of American culture:

Amazing Grace, America (My Country 'Tis of Thee), America the Beautiful, Battle Hymn of the Republic, Blue Skies, Danny Boy, De Colores, Dona Nobis Pacem, Do-Re-Mi, Down by the Riverside, Frere Jacques, Give My Regards to Broadway, God Bless America, God Bless the U. S. A., Havah Nagilah, He's Got the Whole World in His Hands, Home on the Range, I've Been Working on the Railroad, If I Had a Hammer, Let There Be Peace on Earth, Lift Ev'ry Voice and Sing, Michael (Row the Boat Ashore), Music Alone Shall Live, My Bonnie Lies Over the Ocean, Oh! Susanna, Oh, What a Beautiful Morning, Over My Head, Puff the Magic Dragon, Rock-A-My Soul, Sakura, Shalom Chaverim, She'll Be Comin' Round the Mountain, Shenandoah, Simple Gifts, Sometimes I Feel Like a Motherless Child, The Star-Spangled Banner, Swing Low, Sweet Chariot, This Land Is Your Land, This Little Light of Mine, Yesterday, and Zip-A-Dee-Doo-Dah.

"We have a whole generation that has grown up without singing songs like these—songs that are part of our culture, part of who we are," said

Will Schmid, president of the 90-year-old group representing 65,000 music educators nationwide.

Are our churches and church schools doing any better? Are we in our churches singing hymns and songs that are part of who we are? Is it possible to develop a basic list of hymns and songs that are a fundamental part of our Christian heritage, that are basic to who we are as a worshipping community? Is it possible to teach those hymns and songs—one new hymn a week or one new hymn a month—through whatever educational opportunities are available to us in our congregations? Does the repertoire of song we are teaching reflect our particular heritage and identity as Christians?

The place to start is with the hymnal, the book which should properly assume the position of primary importance in the worship and catechetical life of the congregation. Then teachers need to learn how to teach children to sing by singing for and with them.

If congregations are not persistently intentional about teaching and handing on their heritage of Christian song to future generations, the days ahead look bleak indeed. Congregations need to realize that the inconsequential fluff promoted as Christian song and being taught to children in countless schools, Sunday Schools, and parishes is simply not good enough.

The lamentable state of singing in many congregations will not be cured by new and larger sound systems, by "song leaders," or by a frantic search for ever new and faddish repertoires in an attempt to be "relevant and meaningful." It will be cured when congregations patiently, winsomely, and persistently teach the treasury of the church's song to its children and use it regularly in their worship.

The alternative is for silent times ahead—and we shall have no one to blame but ourselves when the song dies out.

# Teaching the Songs of Faith

Who will teach our children the traditional songs of faith?

Past generations did it with a combination of home, school, and church. Songs of faith were learned where families gathered around the piano to sing, in devotions in the parish school and Sunday School, and in church where the treasures of the hymnal were continuously explored.

Today, families seldom gather around the piano anymore, children, we are repeatedly told, can't learn the church's basic treasury of hymns because they are too hard, not particularly suited to children, or just plain not fun enough, and churches are told to get rid of their hymnals in the name of more effective marketing and growth. The result is that in many parishes the historic treasury of the church's song is falling into disuse through neglect and, in some instances, by design.

In both public and parochial schools, many children don't even know the standard Christmas carols. In their place children learn "I saw mommy kissing Santa Claus," "Rudolph the red-nosed reindeer," and other secular songs of the season apparently more suited for children.

The simple reason for this situation is not that hymns and carols are too hard or not enough fun. *The church has failed children by simply neglecting to teach those songs which best nourish and nurture the faith.* Their place has been taken by a variety of "children's songs" which do little or nothing either to nourish the faith or prepare children for participation in the worship of the congregation.

Every teacher knows that there are concepts and skills that children need to be taught at successive stages of their growth. A mathematics teachers worth her salt would hardly say, "Let's skip adding and subtracting this year and do something more fun and more meaningful." She knows that without a solid grounding in basic skills and understandings nothing else will be very meaningful, useful, or even, ultimately, much fun.

*One of the most significant things the church can do to pass on the faith to the coming generation is to teach them a basic core of hymns which the church uses to confess and celebrate the faith.* With good reason, that canon should consist of hymns largely taken from the church's treasury of song from its past, hymns which have stood the test of time, enriched by examples from the church's present. The place to start is with the hymnal. This book reflects a large degree of agreement on a basic core of hymns to be used in worship. But they need to be taught to and learned by each new generation. And they need to be used regularly in congregational worship.

Who will teach our children the songs of faith? Home, school, and church all have a part to play. And unless we are ready to give up a generation with no strong roots in the church's treasury of song, we had better get busy.

# Telling the Story

"Tell me a story!" is the familiar plea as countless young children pick up a well-worn book and hand it to their parents or grandparents, hoping to gain a few more minutes before bedtime. But whatever their motive, children love to hear stories. And they love to hear them again and again.

If your family is like ours, when the children, now all grown, are home, we like to reminisce about all the things—the momentous, and the not-so-momentous—that happened as they grew up. It usually begins, "Do you remember when..." We are telling "our story" as a family, rehearsing our history, recounting what it is that binds us together, what gives us our identity as a family. We don't invent new stories. We tell the old stories. And we tell them again and again.

What we do in worship is essentially the same, "rehearsing our story" as Christians, telling again and again in ritual and song the story of salvation, establishing our identity as part of God's family, finding our place in the long history of God's people of which we and our children have become a part through baptism. We don't—or shouldn't—invent new stories; we tell the old story and attempt to discern its meaning for our lives.

One of the important roles of liturgy, ritual, and song in the Church is to guard the telling of the story so that we don't go our own way and begin telling other stories. A great temptation of our day is the misguided search for novelty in worship, a novelty which usually ends up telling other stories. The greater problem is not that "we've always done it that way before," but getting around the notion that worship which is "new and improved" is bound to be better.

Perhaps we need to recover the innocence of those who know "the story," but participate in the liturgy of the Church with the freshness that comes with hearing the story for the first time. Perhaps it is our loss of innocence that impels us to the fallacious conclusion that in worship we must strive first and foremost to "make things interesting." Perhaps the real problem is not that we have tried the discipline of the liturgy—and it is a discipline—and found it wanting, but rather that we have never before been confronted by the rigorous demands of Christian worship, that we have rejected it without really having tried it at all!

As we "keep our story alive" through the discipline of liturgy, ritual, and song, we renew our participation in a tradition extending both backward and forward in time. And we are a crucial link in the survival of that tradition. When we and our children do not rehearse the story, the chain is broken, and we are cut off from the possibility of inhabiting both the past and the present of "our story." And when cut off from our past story, our newly-invented rituals—no matter how interesting their subject matter or varied their presentation—can share only marginally in that past and in that story.

So here is a vote for telling the story—and the liturgy, ritual, and song by which the story is kept alive. And for telling it again and again.

# Those Ubiquitous Children's Sermons

Children's sermons come in all shapes and sizes. Found in churches large and small, they are often a way for pastors to demonstrate they can "relate" to children. Some are long, some are short. Some are well done, others leave much to be desired. They seem to be cropping up everywhere.

The question is—should they be at all?

One recent Sunday morning, I encountered what was probably a very typical example. The pastor invited the children to join him on the chancel steps. It took a bit of cajoling. "Come on now, don't be bashful." A few apparent "regulars" promptly came forward. Others, not at all convinced, were shoved by their parents into the aisles.

After four or five youngsters had volunteered, the pastor held up a "mystery box" asking what the children thought it contained. The answers, amid occasional snickers and laughter, were almost predictable: a "Nintendo game," suggested one child; "a Teenage Mutant Ninja Turtle," said another; "Jesus", shouted a third, convinced that at last he had the correct answer. What did the box contain? A brand new pair of Nikes—and the pastor proceeded to use it as the basis for an object lesson, something about "running the race." There seemed to be a great sense of relief when it was all over.

Was my experience a caricature of children's sermons? I don't think so.

Somewhere along the line, propelled by enthusiasm for a breezy liturgical style which equates trendy informality and forced ebullience with "participation" in worship, the "children's sermon" seems too often to have crossed the line between what was thought it might be and what it too often has become—entertainment.

The idea of children's sermons undoubtedly springs from the worthy goal of involving children meaningfully in worship. But does it—really?

Do children's sermons really help draw them into what the worship of the whole congregation (including children!) is really all about—God speaking to us and our response in adoration, prayer, and praise?

Do children's sermons place the focus where it belongs? It was clear that the congregation's attention that Sunday focused on the children. Would they blurt out something unexpected and embarrass the pastor or their parents? How would the pastor respond to unpredictable answers?

Do children's sermons too easily settle for "another Gospel"? It was clear that the "message" that day easily slipped into a casual moralizing. "Will Jesus like us if we do this or that?" The implied answer seemed to be "No."

Children's sermons seem to speak volumes about our failure to draw children into meaningful participation with the whole congregation throughout the entire service. Are there more appropriate ways of involving children in the assembly's worship? Can we do better?

I think so. Highlighting one place in worship as "for children" suggests that the rest is somehow irrelevant. Why not help children learn to participate in the *entire service* by teaching the songs of the liturgy, by sharing the stories of the scripture before they are heard on Sunday, by helping children learn the hymns to be sung the next week? These are simple and obvious places to start. But they will help children to experience and participate in the *whole* liturgy, not just in one part— "for children."

# *Tradition! Tradition!*

One day, munching a quick snack with my wife at our local Wendy's, a young man, whom I did not know, sat down at the next table with his three small children. I guessed their ages to be one, three, and five years old. The scene was a familiar one, I thought. "Dad is taking the kids out to lunch; they're giving Mom a little break."

What struck me about their noon-hour expedition—a situation fraught with peril, as any father who has ventured forth on a similar assignment can attest—was the marvelous ease with which they handled this adventure. They ate as neatly as children of their ages could. The older children helped the youngest when he needed it. The three and five-year-old handled the plastic forks and spoons as well as one can, and even engaged in simple conversation beyond the normal "do's" and "don't's" and "be careful's." These children—even at their young age—had learned how to conduct themselves in the public ritual of "eating out."

It all reminded me of another young man whom I know. He is a primary grade teacher. For the past decade or so, quietly and without fanfare, he has been helping six-and seven-year-olds know what to do and how to behave in the public ritual we call "worship."

In the first weeks of each school year he takes his first-grade class into the church, shows them the baptismal font and has them dip their hand into the water, takes them to the altar, shows them the stained-glass windows and tells them the stories they depict in words they can understand. He shows them how to sit in the pews, how to hold the hymnal, how to use the colored ribbons to mark the pages they will use for the hymns and liturgy, how to fold their hands, bow their heads, and make the sign of the cross. He is helping them learn who they are as children of God. In short, he is teaching the tradition of public worship. The fruits of that teaching are evident to anyone who observes those children in their daily chapel services. The instruction that young teacher has been faithfully providing for more than a decade is part of the passing on of the "tradition" of worship.

"Tradition" seems to be a bad word for some. It suggests sameness, repetitiveness, everything contrary to what some adults seem to want: newness, freshness, always something different. Psychologists are closer to the truth when they say that all of us—children and adults alike—

need structure, boundaries, parameters within which we live and work, and worship.

Parents could learn from these first-graders. Martin Luther once remarked concerning the participation of children in worship that " . . . the common people will learn from the pupils what, when, and how to sing and pray in church . . . When the pupils kneel and fold their hands the common people will imitate them."

Perhaps part of the problem with worship is that our children have really learned to do as adults do, not as adults say. What does our example say to children as we attempt to lead them to a more reverent, meaningful worship? In the midst of the recurring fads and short-lived whims that pass for worship, how do we help them keep their balance?

Tevye asked the same question in *Fiddler on the Roof*. "How do we keep our balance? Tradition! Everyone knows who he is and what God expects him to do. Without tradition our lives would be as shaky as a fiddler on a roof."

I thought about this as I saw those three children and their father gather their paper plates, napkins, and other debris from their meal, carefully place it in the trash bin, and go on their way.

And I thought of that first-grade teacher with admiration, thanks, and growing respect.

# Twinkie Tunes
## with a Ding-Dong Theology

"You are what you eat!" is a slogan that has captured widespread interest and attention. Young and old, teenagers and senior citizens, and even children—not disparaging an occasional Twinkie or Ding Dong—are watching what they eat. Junk food is out, healthy is in. Paraphrasing political rhetoric, we say "It's the nutrition, stupid!"

Fed by cries of "This is what we like" or "This is what people want," the church has seen a rise in popularity of its own kind of musical junk food. As a result, a growing repertoire of the musical equivalent of Twinkies is contributing to the serious musical malnourishment of God's people. Characterized largely by musical fluff, this repertoire features insipid melodies set to third-rate imitations of the latest pop trend with texts that range from the theologically simplistic to the simply wrong.

Ralph Vaughan Williams, in the Preface to *The English Hymnal* (1906) had an answer to those who argue that while "fine tunes are doubtless 'musically correct,' . . . people want 'something simple.'" He points out that the expression "musically correct" has no meaning. Rather, the only 'correct' music is that which is beautiful and noble. The issue, he points out, is a moral (we might say nutritional), not a musical, one.

Children need to be nurtured in the faith with more than musical Ho-Hos and textual Twinkies. In many places children—and their parents—no longer know the basic core of the church's hymnody. They simply have never learned—or been taught—it. Instead their teachers opt for "catchy" songs they think children will like and which someone has told them are "more suitable" for children. We shall soon be reaping the harvest of a generation of children whose concept of the church's song has been shaped by the musical equivalent of Twinkies and Ding Dongs.

The church's song is 1) to speak the Gospel clearly and unequivocally 2) through musical vehicles reflecting the character of the Gospel in the honesty and integrity of its craftsmanship. Twinkie tunes and texts fail on both counts. Where we see no textual difference between, for example, Jaroslav Vajda's rich "Christ goes before" and "I have decided to be a Christian," we ignore the first task. Where we see no musical difference between, for example, Vaughan Williams tune *Sine nomine*

("For all the saints") and the latest favorite in the "Twinkie tunes" category, we ignore the second. This is no false choice between populist ("Music for the people's sake!") and elitist ("Music for its own sake!") views. It is rather a concern for music and words for the Gospel's sake.

If it is true that in matters of faith "We are what we sing," and if the present trend continues, then get ready for a generation which knows only "Twinkie tunes" with a theology to match.

# Welcoming Those Other Strangers

Good friends will soon be leaving our congregation, relocating a thousand miles away. They are looking for a new church and are in the process of "church shopping," joining that company of "strangers" that congregations are being encouraged by the gurus of growth to "welcome" these days.

They are leaving a congregation which has enriched their lives and strengthened their family in large part by centering its mission in its worship life, through weekly celebration of Holy Communion, by giving music a significant place in its worship, through excellent Gospel preaching, and the experience of rich and vibrant congregational singing. Their children have grown up in a church and parish school where they have experienced worship which is reverent, broadly participatory, meaningfully related to their lives, and which has brought a welcome continuity and stability in the midst of a culture which relentlessly emphasizes the opposite.

What this family—father, mother, and three teenage young people—is looking for is a congregation which will continue, deepen, and extend those experiences. What they are finding as they "church shop" is a bleak and desolate wasteland.

Many congregations they have visited, gathered in recently renamed "worship centers," seem to them to be centered elsewhere: around the personality of the pastor, or around music as a "performance" by soloists and bands whose effect—intended or not—is to depress, or in many cases simply replace, congregational singing. Holy Communion is infrequently celebrated, and any continuity with the worship tradition of the church is readily sacrificed to the "creative" contributions of its leaders. Zealous to "reach out," they relentlessly espouse the currently popular views of worship as entertainment and the Gospel as a "product" to be "sold," rather than as the announcement of new life for the taking.

Sadly, it seems not to have occurred to these congregations to ask how many people they are turning away by their trendy ideas of relevance. More important, it seems not to have occurred to them to ask whether their approach—in spite of all the talk about evangelism and filling the pews—will ultimately leave our children high and dry, yielding the next generation an evangelical disaster with truly empty churches. They have forgotten the advice of Dean William Inge that

"Whoever marries the spirit of an age will find himself a widower in the next generation."

A recent statistic suggests that a majority of new adult members in most congregations come as "transfers" from other Christian congregations or traditions. Many come from congregations which highly value the tradition of Word and sacrament. That many new converts are attracted to those congregations which value the beauty and integrity of its liturgy and the reverence of its music, seems to go unnoticed or ignored.

Where will such people—who look to enrich their lives and strengthen their families through worship which values tradition, the sacraments, and the stability and continuity which the liturgy provides—go?

Who is welcoming these strangers?

# What Ever Happened to the Numinous?

Christian worship—even at its simplest—has a profound sense of the holy. From Moses at the burning bush to the angels announcing Christ's birth at Bethlehem, from the disciples on the mount of transfiguration to the centurion at the foot of the cross, a sense of adoration, wonder, and unspeakable glory—of the numinous—has been an important part of Christian worship. Before the otherness of God we fall down in wonder, awe, amazement, and praise.

All this, of course, is quite foreign to a culture where few things inspire reverence and awe, and where adoration and a sense of the holy is virtually unknown. Especially in matters religious, reverence, wonder, and awe are in alarmingly short supply these days.

This is particularly true in connection with the tidal wave of "contemporary services" inundating the church these days. By any musical standard few are really "contemporary," and the "service" they render is, at best, questionable. In most all of them, wonder and awe have been jettisoned for immediacy, entertainment, and a commercial approach to worship which, while intending to "reach out," is, I believe, more often "turning off" an increasing number of the faithful as well as those such services intend to attract.

Characterized by earnest, well-meaning, but too often ill-prepared musicians compensating for a lack of competence by intrusive displays of personal piety, by instruments amplified to the point where singing is effectively squelched, by "bands" insisting on being "up front" where they can be seen and duly appreciated by all, and by congregations wrestling with words and melodies they have never seen before, the results of such "contemporary services" are almost always predictable. Encouraged and promoted by church leaders desperately reaching out for anything they think will build attendance, the outcome is almost always an unmitigated disaster.

But whether such services are the work of mediocre amateurs or the polished product of professionals, what is wrong with this picture is that it is out of focus. Where attention should be focused—on the liturgy and the good news of the Gospel—it is not. Where it should not be focused—on performers, on staging, on musical arrangements—it is.

What should be the song of the people becomes a solo performance we are obliged to watch and listen. What should be the proclamation of the Good News is too often a self-indulgent display of personal piety. But music intended as a vehicle for congregational praise and proclamation does not "star" its performers. Attention directed to performers is attention diverted from the liturgy and the Gospel. This is not a question of musical style; it is a question of worship out of focus.

"Contemporary services" need to focus less on its "artists" and "performers," less on the placement of "bands" screaming "Hey! Look us over!," less on over-amplified ensembles which refuse to let us hear the sound of the congregation they are presumably there to lead and encourage, and less on egregious public displays of personal piety.

When a sense of wonder and awe begins once again to find its place in worship, it will be a clue that we are on the way back to a simpler and more profound understanding and practice of worship. Until that time, those promoting "contemporary worship" as the solution to all our problems will, I'm afraid, remain quite clueless.

# What's In a Name

What's in a name?

Perhaps more than meets the eye! Not simply convenient labels, names tell the world who we are! Only after considerable thought do fathers and mothers choose their children's names. Parents exhort their offspring to "live up to" them. ("Remember, Johnny, you are a Schmidt!") Names are a way in which we establish our identity.

How churches name themselves presents a fascinating picture of how congregations view themselves and their mission in their community.

Many congregations are named after heroes of the faith: St. Matthew, St. Mark, St. Peter, St. Paul, among the better known, and St. Michael, John of Beverly, John Hus, among the lesser-known. Martin Luther (among Lutherans, of course) has his share. Such names give opportunity for teaching, learning, and witnessing to the faith, and their choice provides an annual opportunity for celebrating the faith on the festival or commemoration appointed in the church's year.

Not surprisingly, seasons or events in the church's year are celebrated by such congregations named Advent, Ascension, Epiphany, Transfiguration, Resurrection, All Saints, Holy Trinity, or Christ the King Church.

Elaborations on the picture of the Shepherd are popular. There is a Shepherd of the Desert, Shepherd of the Pines, Shepherd of the Mountains, Shepherd of the Hills, Shepherd of the Valley, Shepherd of the Ridge, Shepherd of the Rockies, Shepherd of the Springs, Shepherd of the Bay, Shepherd of the City, Shepherd of the Grove, and Shepherd in the Plains. Another group of congregations take the name of Christ in their title: Christ the King, Christ the Servant, Christ the Vine, Spirit of Christ, Cross of Christ, Glory of Christ, Risen Christ, and just plain Christ Church.

All such names say something about the faith these parishes celebrate!

Then there are those congregations whose names simply suggest geographical location: Inter-Mountain, Town and Country, Mt. Hulda, Sun Lakes, Swede Valley, Escarpment, Vestavia, Clear Lake, Oxon Hill,

Park View, Signal Hill, Rivercliff, Webster Gardens, Rainbow Lake; or other names like First Church—which seem suggests that its founders got there before others, or that "We're number one!" What kind of identity do such names suggest? What do such names project about the witness and beliefs of those congregations?

With a world, and especially its children, desperately in need of heroes and heroines—one looks in vain for churches recalling in their name the faithful witness of women of the church —the Church has countless examples to offer from every age. How we name our churches often reflects the breadth and understanding—or lack of it—of our vision of Christian witness and service.

Are we ready for a church named after St. Barnabas, St. Phoebe, St. Dorcas, a St. Mary Magdalene, or even a St. Mary Mother of Our Lord Church? Time—and the breadth of our vision and understanding—will tell!

# *Woodsman, Spare That Tree!*

It is—to use a good theological term—omnipresent. You see it as a place marker in hymnals and bibles, it serves as a fan when the weather is hot, and as something to scribble on by small children during worship. It ranges from a simple listing of parish events to bloated packets of paper ten and twelve pages thick.

"It," of course, is the "worship folder," the "service program," the "church bulletin," which seems to have become the one indispensable, can't-do-without item for worship. But ask any church secretary about the most onerous weekly task, the one which brings the most headaches, and "preparing the bulletin" wins hands down!

Compounding the problem for everyone—church secretaries and worshippers alike—is the current fad for bloated bulletins which copy out the complete service for each person every week. These "service folders," swollen beyond necessity, is simply another sign that worship has become largely entertainment. "Service folders" have nothing to do with being caught up in the wonder of the prayer life of the community. But just like attending a play or concert, we want to know the cast of characters, the leading man or lady, who is doing what, what piece the choir is singing or the organ playing. As one Catholic critic has remarked, most church bulletins are "the Mass with a menu."

Did Luther pass out "worship folders" at the Castle Church in Wittenberg? Did John Wesley concoct a weekly "church bulletin" so his congregation in Savannah, Georgia, would know what came next? Did C. F. W. Walther and his followers dispatch a church secretary to prepare a "service program" so they could celebrate the liturgy in Perry County?

The answer, of course, is that they—with countless worshipping Christians before them—*knew* the liturgy. If, some Sunday morning, all hymnals and church bulletins mysteriously vanished from our pews, we might be surprised how well most congregations could sing the liturgy from memory. And congregations today that know the liturgy through repeated use find that a service reproduced in detail in a bulletin is not only superfluous, it is counter-productive.

One wonders how many trees are being sacrificed supplying the paper wasted on these bloated "service folders" produced each week only to be thrown away. But the liturgy is not a "worship program" that needs a "service folder" to sustain it. The liturgy is a simple ritual act in which God's people gather around Word and Sacrament and which draws its power as ritual from its regular repetition. It is an action easily committed to memory if we would let it. To achieve *that* end we don't need bulletins, we need intelligent repetition of the liturgy with the emphasis on continuity, not on a mindless and ultimately confusing search for "variety."

Imagine a congregation where the people sing the liturgy largely "by heart." Where people sing the "Lord, have mercy," "O Christ, thou Lamb of God," or "Thank the Lord and sing his praise" from memory. Without a bulletin!

Perhaps its time to think less about preparing elaborate bulletins and more about nourishing a love for the riches of the liturgy among us. Perhaps its time to change that slogan from "user-friendly" to "Woodsman, spare that tree!"

# Worship Through Alice's Looking Glass

What is wrong with these descriptive words or phrases taken from church bulletins describing their parish worship: words like the plain vanilla of "traditional" and "contemporary," phrases like the jazzier but more enigmatic "classic traditional" and "classic contemporary," or perhaps the most intriguing "contemporary traditional?"

The simple answer is that in the topsy-turvy Alice-in-Wonderland world in which much of parish worship today seems to exist, nothing is as it purports to be, none of these terms really says what it means or means what it says. All of them reflect a distortion and misunderstanding of both the church's tradition as well as the idea of the contemporary. As a result, most conversations about parish worship start off with mis-perceptions not always easy to surmount.

The most recent voice in the conversation is the magnificent and lavishly produced four-part PBS series "The Choir." The story by Joanna Trollope pits the choirmaster and headmaster of the choir school at the fictional Aldminster cathedral against the dean and his cronies who wish to eliminate the choir, ostensibly to pay for a new cathedral roof. The dean sees the maintenance of the cathedral's 400-year-old choral tradition as an anachronism, an archaic impediment to the church's work in the modern world, as well as to his apparent ecclesiastical ambitions.

For the dean of Aldminster, the word "tradition" seems to connote—as for many who use it in the present-day "worship wars"—stagnation, inflexibility, and resistance to an open future. In actual fact the Latin *traditio*—from which we get our English word "tradition"—is an *active* word, an *active* concept, it is an *act*, the *act* of "the handing over of something from the past to the future." It is, at the same time, the ballast providing the necessary stability and continuity as Christians move from any present to the future.

At its root, the church's tradition refers to what the church essentially is and does—a community that baptizes, proclaims the Word, celebrates the meal. In a broader context it can include other aspects which assist and support those essentials. From the very beginning, the church's song has been closely allied with what the church is and does.

Do we need the modern-day equivalent of an Aldminster cathedral with its choir? Perhaps. Sixteenth century Lutherans, for example, had them in the form of court chapels and the larger city churches. Luther spoke approvingly of such endeavors and encouraged princes to support them, scolding and reproaching them when they failed to do so. There is no doubt a place for such "cathedrals" today—larger churches with ample musical resources where an understanding and practice of worship and music in the historical tradition is regularly brought to life week after week.

But that tradition needs to be handed on in parishes that would never think of themselves as "cathedrals." It is, in fact, being handed on in countless parishes of modest size and resources where faithful church musicians—quietly and without fanfare—are passing on the living tradition of congregational song; where children are being taught the great hymns of the church on a regular and systematic basis; where with steadfastness and faithfulness pastors, church musicians, choirs, and organists work together to help congregations learn, experience, and grow into the richness and vitality of liturgical worship.

Where this is happening—and it is happening in more places than one might think, the tradition is being handed on and received with gratitude and thanks by succeeding generations. Where it is not, where the tradition is compromised by theologians, declared irrelevant by sociologists, or simply ignored by a variety of the well-intentioned, what is being handed on to our children is not the tradition—"the living faith of the dead," but a barren traditional*ism*—the "dead faith of the living."

And where that tradition is not being celebrated and passed on to future generations, we are back in Wonderland where nothing is as it seems, where words like "traditional" and "contemporary" don't really mean what we think they mean, and where nothing is as it pretends to be.